500
Wild & Wacky
Web Sites

Series Editor: Colleen Collier, Lucy Dear, Nicki Mellows, Nikole Bamford
Research: Nick Daws, Linley Clode, Nikole Bamford
Additional Contributors: Keith Fyfe, Christine Pountney,
Richard Skinner, Sue Curran, Sarah Wells, Ann Marangos
Page Design and Layout: Linley Clode
Cover Design: Stephen Godson

Published by:
Lagoon Books
PO Box 311, KT2 5QW, UK
PO Box 990676, Boston, MA 02199, USA

www.thelagoongroup.com

ISBN: 1906170127

Printed in Thailand.

500
Wild & Wacky
Web Sites

LAGOON
BOOKS

CONTENTS

INTRODUCTION

'The Internet is a tidal wave...drowning those who don't learn to swim in its waves' – Bill Gates

Over the past few years, many guides to the Internet have been written explaining how to access the Net and how to use it. But now everyone's looking for a fun and easy-to-use guide to the best sites, so here it is!

This stunning 282-page directory lists 500 of the Weirdest & Wackiest Web Sites on the Internet and is subdivided into six amazing chapters according to subject to make searching even easier!

The research has been carried out by an avid team of fun-loving Internet surfers whose brief was to find the funniest and most original sites for you to enjoy – which is just what they did! Go to p41 or p143 to see what I mean!

Each site is listed with the web address and several lines of text, hinting at what you might find if you log on and visit the web site. The book is for all ages and abilities – you don't have to be a computer whizz or an Internet expert to use it.

Amongst the 500 fantastic web sites listed here, you will be able to find out...

...Where you can buy a million dollars for just $0.50
...How long you have left to live
...How to build your own computer...from scratch!
...Where your missing socks are hiding
...Whether or not you have been abducted by aliens
...Who owns a container filled
with their own navel fluff
...What garbage top Hollywood stars
have thrown out recently
...Where you can buy a piece of Mars
...Where you can read secret FBI files

It's amazing what people put on the Internet, so here is the ultimate guide to finding all that is silly, funny, ridiculous, creepy, weird and outrageous!

Get online for hours of fun and entertainment!

If it's weird and wacky, you'll find it here!

1

Silly, Funny and Ridiculous

The Subservient Chicken
http://www.subservientchicken.com

What could be more fun and relaxing than ordering a chicken about? Type your demands into the box provided and watch the poultry slave comply.

April Fools Online
http://www.wonderfullywacky.com

Don't know what to buy your boring aunt or uncle? Make their day with a Kung Fu Hamster, Moose Poop Candy Dispenser or Chocolate Body Painting Kit.

Love And Balloons
http://www.balloonhat.com

The home page of a couple of guys, who travel the world to make balloon hats for unhappy people, with photos of people wearing their balloon hats in 34 different countries!

Mondegreen Madness
http://www.kissthisguy.com

Who sang 'The Ants Are My Friends' and what exactly is a Mondegreen? Find out in this madcap list of misheard lyrics.

Cyber Stare
http://www.pixelscapes.com/spatulacity/stare2.htm

So you think you can out-stare anyone in a contest? Try this virtual reality staring contest...

The Mother-of-all-excuses Page
http://members.tripod.com/Madtbone

Divided into categories such as police, school, work, and breaking a date – this site offers a plethora of excuses. Perhaps you will want to submit your own gems?

Guess Who I Am!
http://www.smalltime.com/dictator.html

A simple online game where you pretend to be a sitcom character or a famous dictator and the computer tries to figure out who you are.

How To Get A Baby Without Trying
www.discountbabies.com/

Bid for a baby without the hassle of partners, pregnancy or interfering in-laws.

Pave the Planet
http://www.geocities.com/ SouthBeach/1380/pave.html

This hilarious site has come up with the 'perfect' solution to all of our environmental problems – what do you think it is?

How To Dance Properly
http://www.zefrank.com/invite/swfs/index 2.html

Men, in particular, can be guilty of some extremely bad dancing...but help is finally here in the shape of this hilarious site!

9

The Great Debate Page
http://www.angelfire.com/ct/tpdebate

Which way round should the toilet roll be hung? Which is best – sauce or gravy? A simple voting site on these and other extremely important issues. Make sure you have your say!

The Love Calculator
http://www.lovecalculator.com

'Do you love me 85 per cent?' 'Oh, then do you love me 76 per cent?'. Enter two names into the 'Love Calculator' and find out what your chances really are.

The Guy Card
http://www.guycard.com

Do you feel your right to be a guy is diminished in this modern world? Do you want to reclaim the right to dress like a guy, watch guy TV and generally do guy things? If you answered 'Yes' to any of these questions, you obviously need a 'Guy Card'.

11

Tip a Cow
**http://www.nwlink.com/
~timelvis/cowtip.html**

Real-life cow-tipping is a dangerous and cruel prank – but at this site you can fulfil your desire to tip a virtual cow as many times as you like!

Just Chill Out
http://www.mezzowave.net/chillout.htm

When all the silliness gets too much, take a relaxing breather at the 'super-sensory chill-out lounge' on this cool site, with its cool online ambient music.

Large Furry Animals
http://www.nose-n-toes.com

Llamas aren't cute, are they? But, if you happen to know anyone who harbors the delusion that they are, you can order them any of a huge range of llama-themed merchandize from this site.

Shrink in a Box
http://www.dreamwv.com/ shrink/shrink.html

Don't want to pay by the hour? Need a quick analysis? Visit the site, take a seat, the doctor will be with you shortly...

Python Online
http://www.pythonline.com

The official site of all things relating to the pythonesque world of 'Monty Python'. An absolute must for fans.

Free Cartoons
http://www.joecartoon.com

Download original animated cartoons to watch on your computer. Choose from a huge range, including Disco Mouse, Teenage Gerbil Bikers and Santa Yo' Daddy.

The Movie Nitpickers' Site
http://www.nitpickers.com

We've all seen them – those continuity mistakes, the out-of-sequence scenes where the empty glass has become full. Here's the site where you can register your own movie nitpick, or just peruse the massive archive of what other people have already noticed.

Stare Down Sally
http://www.stairwell.com/stare

Sally will blink...eventually! Do you think you're a match for her?

I Should be Working!
http://www.ishouldbeworking.com

But you're not, are you? Visit this site to enjoy amusing offerings from like-minded slackers.

Apology-note Generator
http://www.karmafarm.com/ formletter.html

This web site takes all the effort out of finding the right words to say you're sorry – and when you're happy with your message, it will e-mail it to your beloved for you!

Useless Facts Page
http://www.amusingfacts.com

Useless facts it promises and useless facts it gives, by the wagon-load! They're arranged in 18 different categories and if it's funny it must be true!

Lose Weight Instantly!
http://www.exploratorium.edu/ ronh/weight

Diet not going well? Cheer yourself up by discovering how much less you'd weigh on Mercury, Venus, Mars, or any other planet in the solar system.

17

The Bureau of Missing Socks
http://www.funbureau.com

Find out more about one of the world's
most frustrating mysteries. A brilliantly
funny and much-needed site
that includes a place
where you can input
details of your own
'single' socks, just
in case the
other one has
been spotted
somewhere in
the world.

18

Uproar!
http://www.uproar.com
Play dozens of free games (some with prizes) at this fun-packed online game show.

Office Pranks
http://www.gwally.com/pranks/office
Liven up a boring day at work by trying out a few of the pranks listed here, from paging a bogus employee to taking a message for your colleague from Mr Bear (with the phone number of the local zoo!).

Thunk!
http://www.thunk.com

Apparently created for kids, this cute online machine will scramble messages for you – hours of fun for the easily amused!

The Anagram Server
http://www.anagramgenius.com/server.html

Type anything in the form and the Anagram Server will find, compute and display all the possible and, often hilarious, results. Hours of fun!

20

Animal Magic
www.switchzoo.com/zoo.htm

Wreak havoc with nature — create your
own bizarre animals

Weird and Funny Stories
http://www.dysan.net/weird/weird.htm

The 25 shortest books ever written, 80
phrases that should be on buttons, the
11th commandment – these are just
some of the short articles to be found at
this amusing site.

The BoomBox Museum
http://www.pocketcalculatorshow.com/boombox

If iPods and mp3 players leave you cold, and you're strangely nostalgic for those old stereos designed to be carried on the shoulder, then this is the site for you.

The Marvels Of Toast
http://www.drtoast.com/recipes.html

Don't just put cheese or beans on it, use your imagination! Here you'll find some extraordinarily exotic recipes featuring, erm...toast.

22

Laugh Till You Cry
http://www.badpuns.com

Groan over the latest puns or peruse past gems in the archives. As the site says — Caution: reading this site may cause quip-lash.

Talk Like a Private Eye
http://www.miskatonic.org/slang.html

You can be talking like Sam Spade within a few seconds of visiting this site dedicated to PI slang. 'The two-bit flim-flammer jumped in the flivver and faded.' Exactly!

23

She's Mine Now
http://www.girlfriendstealer.com

It's not nice but it does happen, so get the lowdown here on girlfriend-stealing before it happens to you. Top tip: Apparently for both genders the number 55 on clothing is a sure sign of a stealer!

Write Like an Egyptian
http://www.upenn.edu/museum/ Collections/egyptian.html

This fantastic site will render your name or any other word you type on the form into colorful Egyptian hieroglyphs.

24

Virtually Man's Best Friend
http://www.virtualdog.com

Perhaps you can't own a real dog due to restrictions of space or time... No problem, get yourself a virtual dog! You'll need to walk, exercise and train it of course... And you can compare how well your dog does with other dog owners!

Purity Tests Online
http://www.armory.com/tests

This 'Adults Only' site lists a large number of Purity Tests that can be found online. List what you get up to and get a 'purity rating'!

Clowns Are Evil
http://www.clownz.com

If big red noses and orange hair scare you, you must visit this site. Read about other people's experiences and explore the twisted world of childhood's worst nightmare...the clown!

One Potato, Two Potato...
http://www.readingtoes.com

Your toes may reveal more about you than you realize. Get the lowdown here from the official web site of the Foundation for Fundamental Dactylogical Reading. Yes, they are serious!

The Toilet Museum
http://www.toiletmuseum.com

'Ladies' Room', 'Men's Room', 'The Great Outdoors', 'Technotoilet' – just some of the toilet information to be found at this site. You can also sign the bathroom wall!

27

Retro Futures
http://www.retrofuture.com

Read what the pundits of the day expected life to be like in the 21st century (leisure 24/7, colonies in the sea, vacation trips to the moon), then ask yourself where it all went wrong.

'Build Your Own Cow' Page
http://members.tripod.com/ ~spows/cow.html

Add legs to the cow, heads, or even change the spots on this wacky page.

The Boring Page
http://www.cavaliers.org/john/boring.html

Fed up with smartass sites that take forever to load and crash your browser? Then pay a visit to 'The Boring Page', which is about as basic as a web site can get!

Inflight Entertainment?
http://www.airsicknessbags.com

Browse through the virtual museum of airplane sickness bags. Choose your flight accordingly.

E-mail's Greatest Hits
http://www.bl.net/forwards

An extensive archive of those amusing and/or pointless e-mails that people forward to each other. Including such classics as 'M&M Duels', 'Prison versus Work' and 'Bedroom Golf'.

Ian's Shoelace Site
http://www.fieggen.com/shoelace/index.htm

Everything you never wanted to know about shoelaces, including how to tie the 'the world's fastest shoelace knot'!

Virtual Food Fight
http://www.foodfighting.com

Start an e-mail food fight with friends or colleagues. Choose from a range of weapons, from spaghetti and meatballs to ice cream sundaes, then splatter away!

The Tongue Twister Database
**http://www.geocities.com/Athens/8136
/tonguetwisters.html**

'Which witch wished which wicked wish' – and a whole list of other tongue-twisters to be tried out right here.

Virtual Bubblewrap
http://www.virtual-bubblewrap.com

We have all done it, popped those bubbles – but isn't it disappointing when they are all popped? Well, here you can find virtual bubblewrap that you can pop forever!

32

Dog Years
http://www.patsyann.com/school/years.htm

This site makes calculation of the above very easy – you can sit and calculate the dog years of your entire family!

Bad Tattoos
http://www.badtattoos.com

Is that supposed to be a rose or an apple? Give your own ratings to some wince-inducingly bad tattoos. Look out for the 'Swiss Cheese' and the 'Clown With Guns' in particular.

33

Live Better, Live Cheaper
http://www.stretcher.com

Even if you think you're good with money, this page 'for professional tightwads' could be a real eye-opener. Read tips here about how to live better for less, and contribute your own.

The Morse Code Translator
http://www.urban75.com/ Mag/morse.html

This site is almost totally useless unless you've always wanted to translate things into Morse Code!

The Virtual Bachelor Pad
http://www.ziggyland.com

Visit the life of a bachelor! Peek inside the bachelor brain or tinker with the bachelor laundry system – if you dare!

The Gallery of Misused Quotation Marks
http://www.juvalamu.com/qmarks

A hilarious site with listings and commentary about 'quotation marks' that 'turn up' in the 'strangest' of 'places'.

Brain Flower
http://www.brainflower.com

Have you ever had a good idea to improve something? This page is full of hilarious and sometimes clever ideas submitted by people just like you!

Spirorama
http://www.thepcmanwebsite.com/ media/spirograph/spirograph.shtml

The 1970s' Spirograph, which created fascinating spiral patterns based on mathematical principles is back and in full color on the Internet!

36

The Traffic Cone Appreciation Society
http://animation.filmtv.ucla.edu/students/awinfrey/coneindex.htm

Lying squashed and forgotten at the side of roads worldwide, this funny site felt there was a need to address the suffering of abandoned traffic cones.

37

The Perfect Present?
http://www.pileofmud.com

Looking for a gift for someone who has everything? This site also offers 'a range of absolutely dire presents', from the woodworm feeder to the teach yourself welly wanging kit.

Web of Lies
http://www.davesweboflies.com

There are nearly 4,000 lies at this site – for example, women are 12 times more radioactive than men! Unbelievable!

38

When Toilets Go Bad
http://home.att.net/~toyletbowlbbs/ toilets.htm

We don't want to hear about it – but we can't help ourselves. Read through tragic news stories of naughty toilets.

The Crate Research and Application Project
http://vzone.virgin.net/ sizzling.jalfrezi/slate/crate

You will simply never know how useful crates can be unless you go find out!

39

Doh!
http://www.dumbwarnings.com

Come here to read no-brainer warnings from businesses across the globe, e.g. the air conditioner that comes with the instruction: 'Caution: Avoid dropping air conditioners out of windows'.

Stupid Adverts From Finland
http://www.saunalahti.fi/~ivanoff/mainos

Who would have thought that the most stupid adverts in the world would come from Finland? View gems like: 'Your Cattle Is Waiting For Phosphate Fodder'.

Computer Stupidities
http://rinkworks.com/stupid

Entertain yourself and feel strangely superior at the same time, as you discover just how stupid some computer users can be.

Find Your Star Wars Twin
http://www.outofservice.com/starwars

Via a short personality test, you can find out if you too are intimately related to a personality featured in Star Wars.

Pet Astrology
http://www.findyourfate.com/astrology/pet-astrology.htm

Pets have star signs too! This page offers you a horoscope reading for your own special animal.

Dancing Pillow
http://www.weebls-stuff.com/games/5/

There are hours of fun to be had causing the cute cartoon pillow to dance using only your mouse.

Facial Furniture
http://members.aol.com/antlavelle

How do you like your sideburns? Big and fluffy or sharp and sleek? This site is dedicated to this dubious facial apparel.

Cliché Finder
http://www.westegg.com/cliche

Need a cliché and need it fast? Over 3,300 cliches are listed and you can search them by keyword to discover (for example) how many include the word 'cat'. Why you would want to is another matter, of course.

The Really Big Button That Doesn't Do Anything

http://www.pixelscapes.com/ spatulacity/button.htm

Some people claim they gain energy or answers – try it for yourself. Push the button that causes nothing to happen. You can even argue with it, if you want.

Angry Gingerbread Men
http://members.iconn.net/~phantom/ginger.htm

Have you got a killer Gingerbread Man tale to tell? Me neither. But plenty of people have... Pictures, stories, oh, and a recipe…

The Dilbert Zone
http://www.unitedmedia.com/comics/dilbert

Read Dilbert comic strips, watch an animated film or find out when he is next on television. You can even get a free Dilbert gift at this official site!

Dancing Paul
http://www.dancingpaul.com

Watch 'Cool Paul' dance to a selection of top disco tracks. You can even choose the scenery in the background!

Flip-book theater
http://www.bigempire.com/postittheater

Remember those mini-films we all made as kids by drawing a series of images in the corner of a notebook and flicking them over? Well, now they're live on the Internet!

The Life of a Hair Ball
**http://mypage.direct.ca/
k/kbotham/hairyindex.html**

The photo-documented story of the
life of a hair ball...the tragedy... the
joy...and the drain!

Online Jigsaw Puzzles
http://www.jigzone.com

Click and drag the pieces to assemble
these virtual jigsaws, from Michelangelo's
David to Tulips in the Rain. Or you could
just get a life instead.

Color It In
http://www.coloring.com

Re-live your childhood with the online coloring books at this site. There are over 100 pictures to choose from, with a new one added each week!

Trivia Heaven
http://www.funtrivia.com

The ultimate site for lovers of all kinds of trivia. Peruse the archives of subjects ranging from 'Animals' to 'Useless Trivia', enter the tournament, or try and answer the trivia question of the day.

Ghost Towns
http://www.ghosttowngallery.com

Are you fascinated by the images of ghost towns in old Western movies, with their abandoned buildings and drifting tumbleweed? Then this site is very definitely for you!

2

Gadgets, Gizmos and Novelties

How Are You Living Without One?
http://www.cycoactive.com/blender

You may have a television, a computer, a car, and lots of other really useful gadgets but do you have...a 'Blenderphone'?

Build Your Own Dalek
http://www.dalekcity.co.uk

Are you a Dr Who fan? Sign up here to learn how to make your very own 'Dalek', then sit back as your creations take over the universe for you...

51

The Lone Zone
http://www.lonezone.com

A solar-powered emergency radio,
a pocket rocket massager, the
Anti-gravity Handbook. A one-stop shop
for bizarre and
hard-to-find items,
gadgets and books
on the Internet.
A must-see site.

Revenge Is Sweet
http://www.revengeunlimited.com

Have you been wronged, mistreated, annoyed or ignored? Get your revenge here, with 'gifts' ranging from a box of melted chocolates to a bouquet of dead daisies!

Rubber Band Shooting
http://hometown.aol.com/morganbolt

Learn the fine points of rubber band shooting at this site. Your office colleagues will look at you with new respect!

53

Feeling Lucky Today?
http://www.7997.com

Where can you find a lucky horseshoe when you need one? This site offers worldwide delivery of authentic horseshoes in gold, chrome and copper.

Take Hoff
http://www.knight-foundation.com/ hoffplane.html

The ultimate David Hasselhoff accessory. Make your very own paper plane in his image.

54

Who Wants To Be a Millionaire?
http://www.themilliondollar.com

Buy your very own million dollar bill for just $0.50.

Android World
http://www.androidworld.com

If making robots that look like humans, but don't complain when they are cleaning the house, is your thing – then this is a great site for you!

I'll Take It!
http://www.aso.com

Need a piston helicopter fast? How about a large transport jet? Visit this aircraft site to find out how much it'll cost you!

Go Gadget Go!
http://www.gadgetsontheweb.com

Divided into hand product sections, this innovative site has something for everyone, from flashlights to touch-screen calculators. Cool!

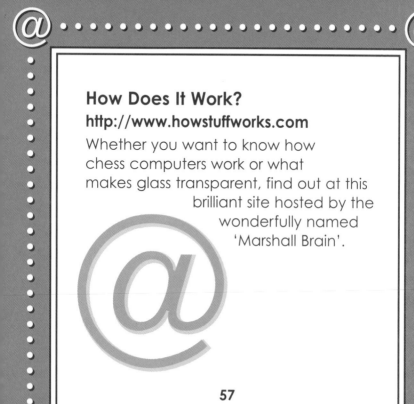

How Does It Work?
http://www.howstuffworks.com

Whether you want to know how chess computers work or what makes glass transparent, find out at this brilliant site hosted by the wonderfully named 'Marshall Brain'.

Bizarre Gifts for Your Pet
http://www.coolpetstuff.com

Does your pooch need an automatic water bowl? Perhaps you would like to strap him into his own motorbike seat. Wacky accessories for pets and humans alike.

My Pet Fat
http://www.mypetfat.com

A weight loss programme that involves carrying around a truly disgusting plastic replica of 1oz of body fat. If that doesn't work, try the 1lb or 5lb mypetfats!

Kope's Gadget Guide
http://www.greatgiftsandgadgets.com

Everything you'll possibly need for that
great gift. Inpiration is here in spades.

The Death Clock
http://www.deathclock.com

Plug your details into the 'Death Clock'
and let it tell you how long you've got
to go!

Kit Planes
http://www.kitplanes.com

Do you dream of having wings? Would you rather visit an airport than a movie theater? If you answered 'yes' to either of the above, then check out this site for lots of tips and info on building your own aircraft.

Bonsai Potato
http://www.bonsaipotato.com

Turn a humble potato into a fabulous sacred bonsai tree! The kit includes pruning shears, tweezers, and a replica altar for your spud.

The Museum of Modern Madness
http://www.madmartian.com

Twisted toward fake horror and science fiction, this site hosts the 'Plastic Eyeball Museum' and other such oddities.

Talking Toilet Paper
http://www.talkingtp.com

A toilet roll holder that plays a message when anyone pulls the paper. Record your own message, or use one from the manufacturer's extensive library of celebrity voices!

Totally Absurd Patents
http://www.totallyabsurd.com

A comprehensive look at the wackier side of inventions – with a huge number of related links and information. Check out the absurd patent of the week – when last checked the featured invention was 'Sleep-no-more Chin Balls'!

Movieprop.com
http://www.movieprop.com

For the low-down on the gadgetry, costumes and other props used in movie special effects, and how to become a collector, visit this fantastic web site.

AIBO – The Robotic Dog
http://www.aibo-europe.com

This incredible robotic dog has its own site, its own fan-club *and* its own magazine – check it out!

Flexi-cardboard records
http://www.wfmu.org/MACrec

Buy your metal and cardboard records here! The site includes lots of recordings for a novelty gift.

Give the Gift of...?
**http://www.nothing.net/
nothing/index.html**

What do you give the person who has everything? The answer is 'nothing'! This site has details about why 'nothing' makes a fabulous gift.

The Duct Tape Guys
http://www.ducttapeguys.com

We have all used it, we know how essential it is to life – but what else do we know about duct tape? This hilarious site offers you duct tape detail, fashion and history!

Uncle Booger's Bumper Dumper
http://www.bumperdumper.com

What is a 'Bumper Dumper'? Well...you could guess!...or you could visit this wacky site to find out!

Gobler Toys
http://www.goblertoys.com

A fantastic site that has to be seen to be believed – offering strange-looking and weird toys, both old and new.

Popular Science
http://www.popsci.com

For the gadget-geek who loves everything with wheels, wings, propellers or hard drives – this is the place for you! All the latest information about what technological marvel is being invented for civilians and the military alike.

Rube Goldberg's
Annual Machine Contest
http://www.rube-goldberg.com

Inspired by the Pulitzer Prize-winning cartoonist Rube Goldberg, famous for his cartoons of wacky contraptions, this site offers the public a chance to enter their own wacky designs into an annual contest.

67

The Ultimate Gadget
http://www.victorinox.ch

How does anyone live without one?
This is the official site of the Swiss Army
Knife – it can do almost anything!

Weird and Wonderful Patents
http://www.lightlink.com/
bbm/weird.html

A small but funny list of bizarre and utterly
useless inventions including floating
umbrellas and jet-propelled trains!

68

Very Cool
http://www.gadgetcool.com/tags/style

Here are the latest cool gadgets - the transparent toaster so you know when it's ready or the armchair that vibrates with the TV action.

Unusual Gifts and Gadgets
http://www.rainbowsymphonystore.com

Anti-gravity toys, aquarium picture frames, unusual yo-yos, dolphin lamps, and a whole host of other gadgets that spin, shine, float and pulsate can be found here.

Gizmo City
http://www.gizmocity.com

An online store offering gizmos for the home and car such as 'Telephone Music-on-hold', a 'No-touch Light Switch' and a 'Wireless Mail Alert' (not for e-mail!)

Pretty Potty
http://www.funkytoiletseats.com

Use these fabulous novelty toilet seats to 'Bring Your Bathroom To Life'. An exotic range of toilet seats in weird and wonderful colours and shapes – including one that opens sideways!

70

The True Blue Roo Poo Company
http://www.roopooco.com

Paperweights and jewellery made from the authentic poo of kangaroos, koala bears and Tasmanian devils. Based in Australia, of course, but willing to ship worldwide!

Could You be a Zorbonaut?
http://www.zorb.com

Take one huge plastic ball, strap a person inside it, roll it down a steep hill...this is where you'll find out everything you ever wanted to know about the Zorb.

71

Memepool
http://www.memepool.com/
Subject/Gadgets

Find a collected list of links to strange gadgets online at this site including a 'disgustoscope'. You ccan also join the hot debate about all things gadget.

Hammacher Schlemmer
http://www.hammacher.com

The true home of strange and, sometimes, useful objects for sale, including gems such as 'Battery-heated Slippers', 'Backyard Dunk Tank', 'Carbon-monoxide-detector Alarm Clock' and an 'Artificial Sun'!

Useless Inventions
http://www.dailygadget.com/

Check out the very latest, most up-to-date gadgets, from the sleekest ipods to the weirdest banana bunkers.

73

Spook Tech
http://www.spooktech.com

Listening devices, night vision, covert spycams and tracking equipment are just a few of the items available at this online spy site.

The Obsolete Computer Museum
http://www.obsoletecomputermuseum.org

Where do computers go when they die? To this site! Check out the interesting exhibition pages.

The T-shirt Mall
http://www.tshirtmall.com

With categories such as 'Terrific and Outstanding Shirts', 'Internet Clothing' and 'Unusual and Bizarre' – this is a great place to find the perfect T-shirt for somebody you love or hate.

The Toilet-seat Lifter
hhttp://www.toiletseatlifter.com/

A one-of-a-kind gadget for boys and girls and hygiene fanatics alike!

Stupid Candy and Pasta
http://www.stupid.com

Computer-shaped pasta, severed finger candy – these and other odd delights can be found at this amusing web site.

Sewdorky
http://www.sewdorky.com

If you can't resist donuts then you'll want your very own hand-made sewn ones. Also available, crocheted teeth if you've lost your own .

Shadow on Gadgets
http://www.spyshops.com

This site features the latest high-tech equipment for use as both 'security and private investigation tools' – they claim they will beat anybody's price on the Internet!

Bioresonant T-shirts
http://www.bioresonant.com

Don't wear dreary black - get some Bioresonant Harmony with these fabulous T-shirts, designed with colour healing in mind. The Bioresonant woven cotton shirts have the added advantage of making your arms happy too!

3D Glasses
http://www.3dglasses.net

Never be short of 3D glasses when you need them ever again! This great site has a huge range for you to choose from.

Tekkie Gadgetry
http://www.topixonline.com

Lots of things that flash, whistle, compute and commute here. The categories include toys, security, nostalgia, health and fitness and many more.

Neo-science
http://www.necrobones.com/neosci

This unusual site takes a look at the weird side of science – offering products and information on bizarre theories and scientific inventions.

The Robot Store
http://www.robotstore.com

Do you want to build a kit robot? This online store might be the place for you to start.

Spam Gifts
http://www.spamgift.com

Range of gifts relating to the famous and much loved canned meat from the Department 56 Spam Museum. Spam golf balls, spam 3D magnets and even a spam casserole dish! What more could you want?

The Chi Machine
http://www.chimachineusa.com

This strange health gadget claims to give you a 'Chi Rush' whilst it aligns your spine, improves your circulation and fixes your 'energy'.

Action Figures
http://www.toypresidents.com

They talk, they pose and they can pose a choking hazard! Get your very own political action gigue, American Presidenst at their very best.

The Museum of Questionable Medical Devices
http://www.mtn.org/quack

A foot-powered breast enlarger, an electric machine to increase virility, soap that washes away the pounds – just a few of the wacky inventions that can be found at this fascinating site.

82

The Cauldron
http://www.thecauldron.com

Spell kits, statues, goblets and cauldrons are just a few of the 'spooky' accessories you can find at this mystical online store.

The 100 Greatest Comics
http://www.geocities.com/ Area51/Aurora/2510/greatest_comics

Who are your favorite comic superheroes? This web site lovingly gives you the details of the top 100.

83

Caught Napping?
http://www.napping.com

Are you in need of napping information and snoozing accessories? If so, then this site was made just for you...if you can stay awake long enough to find it...(yawn).

Build your own PC!
http://www.buildeasypc.com/

It's easier than you think. This site gives you comprehensive instructions on how to build your very own PC from scratch.

84

Home Improvement
http://www.diynet.com

A good general resource for advice, tips and connections to other home-improvement enthusiasts – the page for Mr or Mrs Fixit in your family.

Digital Typing Monkey
http://www.softpedia.com/get/Others/Fun/Infinite-Monkeys.shtml

Can a virtual monkey randomly banging on a keyboard produce the complete works of Shakespeare? Download simulation software here.

Science Gear
http://www.amazing1.com/

This futuristic site features the ultimate modern 'devices' including High Energy Pulsers and Electronic Fishing Aids.

Gadget News
http://www.wired.com/news/gizmos

Get up-to-the minute news on the latest high-tech gadgets and gizmos (including some that don't work!) from the irreverent *Wired Magazine*.

Turtle Art
http://www.turtlekiss.com

Artworks by the world's only professional turtle artist, Koopa. You can buy Koopa's original artworks or commission something brand new. Koopa doesn't care. Koopa is a turtle.

Alien Abductions Inc.
http://www.alienabductions.com

Feeling left out in the abduction stakes?
Wonder why aliens haven't picked you?
This funny site offers 'genuine' abduction
memory implants – out of this world!

See by Night
http://www.night-vision-goggles.com

Turn night into day with the range of
night-vision binoculars, monoculars and
goggles available from this site. Pretty
cool.

Chindogu
http://www.chindogu.com
Chindogu means literally 'weird tool',
and a growing range can be found
here – from the backscratchers' T-shirt to
duster-slippers for cats!

007 Gadget Lab
http://www.geocities.com/
Hollywood/5727/q_lab.html
A brilliant site for descriptions of all the
objects Q invented, including a snorkel
attached to a seagull!

The Spy Tech Agency
http://www.spytechagency.com

Everything you need to become
a spy – all the info and equipment, plus
you can train with them from home!

Tattooed Clothing
http://www.naturalexpressions.org/
Tattoo_Sleeves_Shirts.html

The realistic illusion of tattoos without
any of the pain or commitment. Just
pull on a 'tattoo shirt' and it will look as
though your arms are covered with
ornate tattoos.

Aquatic Bicycles
http://www.americanartifacts.com/smma/velo/velo.htm

If you always wanted to know about bicycles that could travel on or through water then this is the best place to look.

What's That Buzzing?
http://www.rctoys.com

On those rainy days when the TV just isn't enough – be the couch-pilot of a small flying airship. This nicely designed site also offers 'shiny, flying objects'!

Believe it or not!

http://www.amazon.com/exec/obidos/ tg/detail/-/0439417678/103-7766513- 7924629?v=glance

Robert Ripley explored more than 200 countries seeking all things bizarre and extraordinary. Buy this book packed with the weirdest, most outrageous inventions he could find! But only if you love the weirder side of gadget life.

Inventive
http://www.inventing.com/eflp/0/pid72866/D284706/C2238006

A web site with links to tomorrow's inventions for you today! Includes the campocatcher (talking fishing rod) and tips on creating your own.

Futureshock
http://www.internetbrothers.com/futureshock.htm

Find out what will replace computers and how we will use technology to interact with the world.

Veronica's Gadgets
http://www.veronica.co.uk

Serious music gear, such as transmitters and amps, can be found at this online broadcasting equipment store.

Celebrity Gear
http:// www.heavenandearthandyou.com/
Fancy owning a prop or gear that belonged to someone famous? Well, this is the place to purchase it!

Fly Power
http://www.flypower.com

Have you ever wondered if you could tap the energy of a fly to power a light aircraft? For details on how this is done and much more, visit this site. If you've never wondered and think it's a disgusting idea – there is a place on the site where you can voice your opinion.

95

3

Strange and Mysterious

In Search of Atlantis
http://flem-ath.com

A nice introduction site to the famous myth of the drowned city.

The Academy of Remote Viewing
http://www.probablefuture.com

If you want training in how to utilize mind technologies to 'view' locations in other parts of the world, or if you just want to read up about this conspiratorial technology, then this site is for you.

Feral Children
**http://www.feralchildren.com/
en/index.php**

All about children who have been raised
by animals: wolves, most commonly,
although some have called gazelles,
kangaroos and even bears, 'mom'.

The Jackalope Conspiracy
http://www.sudftw.com/jackcon.htm

The Jackalope is said to be one of the
rarest animals in the world. But does it
really exist? Visit this site for more
information and a photo of the elusive
creature.

The Supernatural World
http://www.thesupernaturalworld.co.uk

Vast, multi-award winning site looking at the supernatural, paranormal and unexplained phenomena. Particularly good for the mysterious creature 'Spring Heeled Jack'.

Fainting Goats
http://www-personal.umich.edu/ ~jimknapp/goats.html

Goats that faint? You must be kidding! But no, you can learn all about these rare goats at this site. Boo! Baa! Slump!

99

Strange News!
http://newsbop.triqi.com

A typical strange story on this site is, 'Owners baffled by globe-trotting pig', about a stone pig that one day vanished from its owner's garden and ever since then has been sending her postcards from around the world! Weird!

Spinetingling!
http://www.prairieghosts.com

Explore the haunted history of America with author Troy Taylor and the American Ghost Society.

Voices on Tape
http://www.mdani.demon.co.uk/ stunt/jun97s1.htm

This site is devoted to the mysterious 'spirit voices', which can sometimes be heard on tape recordings, even if no one was speaking at the time. Learn all about the phenomenon here.

Kirlian Photography
http://www.kirlian.org

A camera is offered on this site so that you can take your own 'aura' photographs – what color is yours?

Deathbed Visions and
Out-of-body Experiences
**http://www.healthsystem.virginia.edu/
internet/personality/studies**

The University of Virginia explores
case studies on this web
site – including
out-of-body
occurrences and
children who
claim to
remember
previous lives.

102

Levitation
http://www.hfml.sci.kun.nl/hfml/levitate.html

This small but informative site takes a scientific look at the three main types of levitation.

Cryptozoology
http://www.cryptozoology.com

An online resource for mysterious animals with pictures and up-to-date news of sightings.

103

Who You Gonna Call?
http://www.ghostweb.com

Call the International Ghost Hunters Society. Marvel at pictures and listen to spoo-o-o-ky voices. You can also buy Ghost Hunting for Beginners – an invaluable guide!

Borley Rectory
http://www.prairieghosts.com/brectory. html

Get the lowdown here on 'Borley Rectory', said to be 'the most haunted house in England'. Eerie!

104

Haunted Houses
http://www.english-inns.co.uk/ HauntedInns.htm/

Fancy staying overnight in a haunted castle in, or maybe a long weekend in one of England's haunted inns? Check this site out.

Info Wars
http://www.infowars.com

Check out the news behind the news! This interesting web site has loads of articles and links about politics, religion and world events.

Reverse Speech
http://www.reversespeech.com

What are we *really* saying when we talk to someone? This fascinating site explains 'Reverse Speech Technology' and offers examples of famous people's speeches played backwards!

Mummy Is A Mummy Now
http://www.summum.org /mummification

Burial and cremation is all very well, but the classier way to enter the Afterlife is surely mummification? Treat yourself for around $67,000.

The Reptilian Agenda
http://www.davidicke.com

Ex-soccer goalkeeper turned conspiracy theorist David Icke's home page. Learn about the reptilian aliens' plans for us, see what you think of the future New World Order and much, much more.

The Skeptic's Dictionary
http://skepdic.com

For believers and non-believers alike, this site offers many fascinating, skeptical articles about a wide range of supernatural phenomena and myths.

Nostradamus Online
http://www.nostradamusonline.com

This site offers the original writings of the
famous predictor Nostradamus, as well
as articles, news and other links.

Paranormal Search Engine
http://www.paraseek.com

This is a search engine and links site for
the paranormal and unusual. Use it to
search the web for paranormal sites, or
read about real-life paranormal
occurrences on the 'Investigations'
page.

The Mystical Ball
http://www.mysticalball.com

Pick a number that corresponds to a shape, place your mouse over the mystical ball and the Virtual Wizard will tell you the shape you're thinking of. Telepathy or clever programming? You decide.

Near-death Experiences and the Afterlife
http://near-death.com

Visit this site to read about other people's experiences in near-death situations.

The End of the World – Not!
http://www.abhota.info

Fed up listening to the voices of doom and destruction? Cheer yourself up at this site by reading over 400 end-of-the-world predictions that failed to materialize, the earliest from 2800 BC!

Fortean Times
http://www.forteantimes.com

Unusual news site based on the magazine of the same name, featuring worldwide articles and eager to receive reports from people just like you!

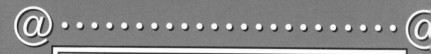

Ghost Village
http://www.ghostvillage.com

Not so much a web site, more a
community of folk interested in ghosts.
There's even a 'Ghost Village'
noticeboard, where
you can post your
supernatural photos
and discuss orbs
and ectoplasm!

111

The Museum Of Unnatural Mystery
http://www.unmuseum.mus.pa.us/unmain.htm

The exhibition halls of this online museum include Cryptozoology, UFOs and Weird Geology. Also includes an Ask The Curator feature. Spooky.

Demon Adoption
http://www.adoptademon.net

Not satisfied with a donkey or penguin? Now you can adopt a demon using this helpful site! Simply select the demon you wish to adopt, save it to your hard drive, register it and away you go!

112

Conspire
http://www.conspire.com

Visit 'Conspire' to see what's available to buy on the bookshelves under the heading 'Conspiracy'.

Yoga – The Cosmic Force
http://www.aetherius.org

This site helpfully explains the connection between the science of Yoga, the theology of all major religions and the mystery of UFOs. In case you had ever wondered...

Sacred Geometry
http://www.intent.com/sg

Find out on this fascinating site how the principles of geometry are reflected in nature. You can learn how the Nautilus shell uses a spiral generated by 'a recursive nest of Golden Triangles'!

Nessie Lives!
http://theshadowlands.net/serpent.htm

A rich site including amazing real-life photos and details of unknown sea creature sightings around the world. See it to believe it!

114

Sarah's Arch Angels
http://www.sarahsarchangels.com

Angel visions, angel pictures, angel rituals, angel poetry, and angel crafts and gifts. The whole angelic shebang.

Strange Magazine
http://www.strangemag.com

The online version of the off-line magazine of the same name - taking an objective look at strange and unusual phenomena.

The World of Unicorns
http://www.geocities.com/
Area51/Corridor/5177

This site offers art, quotes and links about the mythical one-horned horse – you can even adopt your own unicorn!

The Earth Files
http://www.earthfiles.com

A site devoted to strange environmental phenomena, including a good deal about crop circles. Includes the strange tale of 29,000 disappearing pelicans.

116

AIR Magazine
http://www.improb.com

This site deals with improbable research and calls itself the 'MAD Magazine of Science'. You can browse through the ezine online or subscribe to the off-line version.

Apocalypse Now?
http://www.mt.net/~watcher/new.html

This site is dedicated to theories and prophecies forecasting the end of the world, including conspiracies and information relating to the Bible and UFOs.

Ask Bob!
http://www.resort.com/
~banshee/Misc/8ball/index.html

Facing a tough decision? The mystical smoking head of Bob is here to help. Just enter your question, and wait for the oracle to answer in a puff of pipe smoke!

118

Crop Circles
http://www.cropcircleconnector.com /index2.html

All the very latest crop circle photos, news and links. If it's weird and it sprang up overnight, it's likely to be on this site!

The Werewolf Page
http://www.werewolfpage.com

Do werewolves really exist? Browse through the articles and case studies at this thought-provoking site to help you make up your mind.

Weird Encyclopedia
http://www.occultopedia.com/topics/creatures.htm

Whatever weird and wonderful topic you want to know about, from the Abominable Snowman to Zombies, the chances are you'll find it on this site.

Naked Dancing Llama
http://www.frolic.org

Really! The Naked Dancing Llama will answer anything and give you a laugh to boot.

120

World Mysteries
http://www.world-mysteries.com

Well-presented site dealing with lost civilizations, ancient ruins, sacred writings, unexplained artefacts, science mysteries and alternative theories.

Frightening Facts
http://www.ebaumsworld.com/ ghosts.html

Mini documentary which covers ghost photography, ghost videos and electronic voice phenomena... complete with a funky, spooky soundtrack.

Strange and Mysterious

Dowsing
http://www.skepdic.com/dowsing
Dowsing the art of searching for hidden things (water, precious metals etc) using senses we're not even aware of! Learn more here.

The Telepathy Pages
http://www.psychics.co.uk/telepathy.html
Find out about the method of mind-to-mind communication that parapsychologists call telepathy.

Dis-info-mation
http://www.disinfo.com

All sorts of conspiracy articles and theories about modern life, including articles from big names such as Robert Anton Wilson, are to be found on this fascinating and informative site.

The CIA – The Secret Team
http://www.ratical.com/ratville

An online book about America's foremost secret agency – if you are interested in political conspiracy theories, this is a must-read!

123

The FBI
http://foia.fbi.gov

Thanks to the Freedom of Information Act, you are now welcome to browse through the public reading room of the FBI – enjoy!

20/20 Vision for Peace
http://www.2020vision.org

A serious site dealing with environmental issues such as air pollution, toxins and over-population. Read the tips about grassroot activism or learn how to tap into the media for your cause.

124

Scientists and the Paranormal
http://www.issc-taste.org

An online magazine that delves into the strange and mysterious experiences of scientists. Their hope is that through the sharing of information we will better be able to understand the complexities of the human mind.

Astrology and Numerology
http://www.astrology-numerology.com

Learn about these twin mystic arts at this impressively detailed site. Use your new knowledge to help understand your true potential and decide the best times for major moves and activities in life.

In Search of the Giant Squid
http://seawifs.gsfc.nasa.gov/squid.html

Do these impressively large eight-legged monsters really exist? This might help you make up your mind!

Stigmata Through the Ages
**http://www.crystalinks.com/
stigmata.html**

This site briefly lists the famous stigmata
cases in history.

The Psychic Investigator
http://psychicinvestigator.com

This nicely designed site puts the most
popular paranormal events into a
timeline. A good introduction to the
most famous cases of our time,
including those of Uri Geller and Harry
Houdini.

127

Round in Circles
http://www.circlemakers.org

Crop circles – are they evidence of life from other worlds? This site dispels the myth and features a guide to creating your own.

Keys to Consciousness
http://www.themystic.org

Explore the mystical part of your life written by the 'internationally recognized master mystic', Graham V. Ledgerwood. Thirty-two life lessons in higher consciousness can be studied here.

128

Glossary Of The Paranormal
http://www.ufopsi.com/glossary/glossary.html

More an encyclopaedia than a glossary, this site has a very comprehensive list of all the words, acronyms, study centres, key figures and places that relate to the paranormal and UFOs.

Lightning Strikes
http://www.disastercenter.com/lightng.htm

Everything to do with this powerful natural force...

129

Hauntings

http://www.ghosts.org

With a huge archive of stories collected
from the Net and info on lots of specific
haunting cases, this page is a must for
anyone interested in ghouls.

The Truth Is Out There

http://serpo.org/

From 1965-78 a top secret exchange
took place where 12 US military
personnel went to Serpo, a planet of
Zeta Reticuli. This site covers confidential
documents about this program – no
kidding!

Fixed Earth
http://www.fixedearth.com

If you thought money made the world
go round, you're wrong – nothing does.
It's fixed. Suspended between a couple
of giant magnets. And it doesn't go
round the sun either. That fool
Copernicus led us all a merry dance.

The Atlantis Project
http://oceania.org

All about a new Atlantis – a floating city
to be named Oceania. Plans are
currently stalled, but who knows? There
may yet be a flood of interest.

131

Chupacabra
http://www.elchupacabra.com/
Here are theories and info on the
legendary goat-mutilating creature.
Real or fake? You decide.

The Psi-dream Archive
**http://members.aol.com/
DreamPsi/archive**
This fascinating site offers lots of info
about shared dreaming and psychic
dreams, and there's also an online
mutual dreaming class that you can join.

132

Near-death Studies
http://www.iands.org

Read other people's accounts of near-death experiences, submit your own, browse the general info or even join the organization.

More Combustion
http://theshadowlands.net/mystery.htm

This site offers a summary of some reported and photographed cases of this nasty phenomenon – also includes some helpful links.

The Chinese Oracle
http://www.iching.com

The 'I Ching' is the Chinese oracle of changes, and on this site you can get a free reading. Just type a few words about your current situation or relationship, then click your mouse over the sacred pool to see what the stones reveal!

134

The Anomalist
http://www.anomalist.com

A fascinating online magazine dealing with scientific anomalies, unexplained mysteries and unexpected discoveries, such as vanishing hitchhikers and mass suicides.

Prophecies Uncovered
http://www.suite101.com/links.cfm/prophecy

A good place to start a search for info on all forms of prphecy and prediction, including ancient and biblical ones!

135

Weird Magic
http://grindshow.com/GrindShow/fooler tainment.html

Doug Higley's Dark Museum has exhibits for everyone from lovers of the bizarre to buskers. Has to be seen to be believed.

Nessie's Grotto
http://www.simegen.com/writers/nessie

This is the nearest thing to a home page for the Loch Ness Monster. Read all about the legendary creature, including descriptions and photos of recent sightings.

Unexplained Mysteries
http://www.unexplained-mysteries.com

This site describes itself as the online
interactive encyclopedia of the
unexplained. Whatever you're
interested in, find out all about it here.

PCP
http://pespmc1.vub.ac.be/Default.html

Attempting to 'tackle age-old
philosophical questions with the help of
the most recent cybernetic theories and
technologies', this site includes
memetics and ethics.

Sleep Paralysis
http://www.trionica.com

Often thought to be an alien abduction experience, a surprising number of people suffer from this torment. Visit to find out more!

The STATS Spotlight Archives
http://www.stats.org

An interesting web site that examines the true statistics behind government claims and news stories, including GM food production.

Bigfoot
http://www.bfro.net

Read through the theories and sighting reports, or pick up tips on tracking and collecting evidence at this site about the elusive big and hairy one.

The Shroud of Turin
http://www.shroud.com

The best place on the Net to go if you want more details on the famous shroud. Look at photos, read the articles and theories, then make up your own mind about its authenticity.

Wasting Time!
http://members.tripod.com/BabelOnline

Packed full of strangeness and bizarre
facts, this kooky site has been wasting
your time since 1995! Find out more!

Weird Mysteries
http://www.europa.com/
~edge/weird.html

This great site has it all – mysteries that
are to be found on earth, in the air, in
space, and even underground! You
need never search again.

Strange But True
http://www.geocities.com/ mikey_wbt/wbt.html

Mike Boyle has spent years assembling a massive collection of stories that in some way highlight the absurdities of human life. Now he's decided to publish it on the Internet. Read and be amazed!

Two by Two
http://www.arksearch.com/index.htm

You've watched Raiders of the Lost Ark, now read the true story and take a virtual tour of the Ark itself!

141

4

Far Out

Dead Sites
**http://www.disobey.com/ghostsites/
2004_05_19_archive.html**

Where do websites go to die? Ever
wonder what happened to Jennicam or
Angryman.com? Look no further.

Dumb Crooks (aka Mentally
Challenged Criminals)
http://www.dumbcrooks.com

Crooks aren't always the smartest
people in the world. Visit this sidesplitting
site to find out just how stupid they can
actually be.

143

Sandcastle Central
http://www.sandcastlecentral.com/index.html

For serious sandcastle connoisseurs! Tips, news, contests and fascinating photographs of elaborate sandcastles.

Best in Show
http://www.worldbeardchampionships.com/index.html

The World Beard Championships are held every two years. But if you think your own beard is pretty handy and you want to enter, you'll face stiff competition – just check out some of the beauties here!

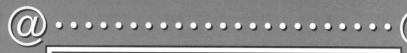

The Origins of the Universe Archive
http://www.talkorigins.org

This site explores the great 'Creation versus Evolution' debate and offers lots of background information for those who are new to the topic.

Purely Purple
http://www.purple.com

If you like the color purple, this is definitely the site for you. Just don't expect very much else!

145

The Weekly Onion
http://www.theonion.com

One of the Internet's best parody newspapers. This product is definitely worth browsing.

The Amazing 'Send Me a Dollar' Web Site
http://server.tt.net/send-me-a-dollar

It's amazing what people use the Internet for. Give this guy a medal! Check out how many dollars he has already accumulated – you won't believe it.

146

Floaty Pens
http://www.5th-sun.com/fpotw

Floaty pens are high-quality souvenir items that are sold worldwide; they're made in Denmark by the Eskeson Company. Marvel over the Buckingham Palace pen and the Graceland, then contact other collectors to trade yours!

Decimal Birthdays
http://www.decimalbirthday.com/index.htm

Need an excuse for a party? Enter your birth date and this site will calculate your next decimal birthday. Now you can celebrate every 1,000 days of your life.

The Incredible World of Navel Fluff
http://www.feargod.net/fluff.html

How much belly button fluff do you think one person can collect in a jar in a year? This site claims to show you the record-holder. Useful, eh?

The Bad Fads Museum
http://www.badfads.com

Silly fashion, ridiculous sports and toe-curling past-times, plus much more from this site. Visit if only to remind yourself of the embarrassment you thought you'd left far, far behind.

The Museum Of Bad Art
http://www.museumofbadart.org

Are those ice creams or mountains? Countless examples of what happens when amateurs express themselves through the medium of paint.

Disco Fever
http://www.70disco.com

A web site entirely devoted to 1970s disco music. Profiles of bands, charts from the 1970s, and more!

Dean and Nigel
http://www.deanandnigel.co.uk

Dean and Nigel demonstrate how to blend in with ordinary members of the public. View their hilarious galleries, which show them 'blending in' with a range of bemused-looking people on Britain's streets!

Ken White's Coin-flipping Page
http://shazam.econ.ubc.ca/flip/index.html

Flip a coin and read the statistics on the coins already flipped – so just how many did come up heads anyway?

I Have the Bends!
http://www.contortionhomepage.com

Some people like to knit or fish in their spare time and some people like to do this! Ouch! Bet they always win 'Twister' though!

151

Fighting Ignorance
http://www.straightdope.com

'Fighting ignorance since 1973 (It's taking longer than we thought)'. Cecil answers all your strange and ignorant questions with quiet patience and cool reason. Is it true that elephants never forget? Why did Kamikaze pilots wear helmets? Find out here.

152

Dumb Laws
http://www.dumblaws.com

Taken from nations all around the world, this web site has archived laws that don't seem to make a whole lot of sense, for example, did you know that in Minnesota it is illegal to cross the state line with a duck on your head?

Toothpaste World
http://www.toothpasteworld.com

Have you ever tried to brush your teeth with chocolate? One man's collection of toothpastes from around the world. And more toothpaste-related fun.

153

Strange Finds
http://www.pavementgear.com

This site is dedicated to strange items found on the roadside, from Santa's hat to a pair of slacks with all the belt loops removed. We can only wonder how they got there!

The Museum of Dirt
http://www.wbur.org/special/strangemuseums/dirt.asp

Jars and jars of dirt. People have sent them from all over the world and some real celebrity dirt. A must-see!

The Cabbage Converter
**http://www.geocities.com/
Heartland/Plains/2144**

Have you ever thought to yourself,
'Gee, I wish I were a cabbage'? Well,
now you can be! Check this site out to
see how!

Modern Moist Towellette
Collecting
**http://members.aol.com/
MoistTwl/gallery.htm**

Don't believe it? Check out the gallery
for yourself – it features a whole array
of damp little tissues!

155

'I Quit!'
http://www.iquit.org

Do you need some help e-mailing your boss? Do you want to see what has happened to others who have quit their jobs in ferocious moods? Visit this site to explore these questions and chat about your own lousy job!

And Adam Knew Eve
http://www.hobrad.com/and.htm

A comprehensive and amusing A–Z list of all the references to sex that can be found in the Bible.

TV Eyes
http://www.tveyes.com

This incredible site offers to e-mail you when a word of your choosing is spoken on television – why don't you try it for yourself.

The Plane Crash Database
http://www.planecrashinfo.com

Browse to find plane crash data in your area or read through the 100 worst aviation accidents.

The Universe of Bagpipes
http://www.hotpipes.com

Everything you did and didn't want to know about bagpipes! The site includes an interactive gallery of various bagpipes that will play music if you ask them nicely!

Juggling Info
http://www.juggling.org

The only place to go if you are interested in juggling, including news, articles, links to juggling clubs and more.

Underground Animals
http://www.animalsontheunderground. com

The London Underground is full of escaped animals! First an elephant was spotted, then birds, cats, dogs... See if you can find a new species.

Earth-cam
http://www.earthcam.com

The huge number of 'cam' categories available on this page include science-cams, restaurant-cams, scenic-cams and religious-cams. Smile, you're on candid cam-era!

Brain Collection
http://brainmuseum.org

A comprehensive, if not a little unsettling, university collection of brains. Big ones, small ones, human and animal grey-matter are all on show at this site.

Grass-Cam
http://www.watching-grass-grow.com

Enjoy watching paint dry? Then you'll love this – a place for the easily amused. Visit this site to while away your time by watching grass grow.

Ultimate Taxi
http://www.ultimatetaxi.com

Why bother catching a cab to go to the local nightclub when the cab is the nightclub, complete with glitter ball and disco lights. Space is limited though – not for the John Travoltas of this world!

161

The Latest Works
http://www.ritsumei.ac.jp/~akitaoka/
saishin-e.html

A web site full of optical illusions
designed to make your head spin.
Examples include The
Chameleon,
Rotating Snakes
and The Packed
Cans. They really
do appear to
shift, spin and
wobble.

The Nose Page
**http://www.well.com/
user/cynsa/nosepage.html**

Add to the many photographs of noses already on the site by sending them a photo of your own hook, snub or ski-jump!

The Web-page Shredder
http://www.potatoland.org/shredder

The web 'shredder' lets you input an url of your choice – allowing you to become a web Picasso via unwanted web waste.

163

Hell Hath Gnome Fury
http://www.bifrost.com.au/hosting/gnomes/

Feeling a tad violent or if you've ever felt the need to be vicious to a garden gnome!This is the place to be.

Roadside America
http://www.roadsideamerica.com/vortex.html

A guide to offbeat roadside attractions across the USA. The controversy over who has the world's largest chair rages on.

Woesome Websites
http://www.webpagesthatsuck.com

How not to create your own website. A list of the worst sites on the web.

Cooking By Numbers
www.cookingbynumbers.com

Just fill out the 'what's in your fridge?' and 'what's in your cupboard?' sections and the site does the rest – producing a list of possible recipes from the ingredients you have. Then get cooking!

165

Far Out

The Multicultural Web Recycler
http://recycler.plagiarist.org

This interesting site scrambles images from web-cams around the Internet and blends them into a work of art.

Mister Cyborg
http://www.cyborgname.com

Enter your name, choose a cyborg avatar, and get a whole new cyborg identity. If you like the sound of your cyborg name, you can use the graphic on your own web site or buy T-shirts and mugs with your new name printed on them.

Freespeling (with one "l")
http://www.freespeling.com

Apparently only 17% of native English speakers can spell properly, so this website campaigns to make certain English words easier to spell. You can vote for new spellings that you think would make life easier - like 'unconshus', 'garantee' and 'axident'.

Ask Doctor Toy
http://www.drtoy.com

Do you want to find out more about the most popular toys on the market? Doctor Toy is the best place to go for the low-down on little people (and big people!) and the gadgets that make them happy.

Eric Harshbarger's LEGO Pages
http://www.ericharshbarger.com/lego

Eric loves LEGO! See pictures here of some of his best creations, like the DNA double helix and life-size, functional grandfather clock!

The Language Kit
http://www.zompist.com/kit.html

JRR Tolkein did it. You can too! This is a very detailed guide to creating your very own language. Easy when you know how!

The White House
http://www.whitehouse.gov

The official site for the home of the US President. Handy if you want to keep your finger on the pulse of US politics – or if you want to send the President an e-mail!

Missile Base Road
http://www.missilebases.com

This site explores the concept of Missile Bases as 20th-century homes and has details of real bases for sale; have you got $300,000 spare?

The Payphone Project
http://sorabji.com/livewire/payphones

This web site invites you to submit a real payphone number from anywhere in the world. There is already a list of such numbers here – so make a call and see who answers!

170

Poor Fluffy!
http://froggy.lbl.gov/virtual/

This interactive site allows you to dissect a digital frog and there are links to serious info on frog biology.

Population Counter
http://www.census.gov/ipc/www/ popclockworld.html

A simple page that does just what it says. When last checked the world population was 6,590,792,270 – wonder what it is now?

Transhumanism Resources
http://www.aleph.se

Transhumanism is about the
future evolvement of human beings,
including uploading human
consciousness into
computers, and
life-extension
techniques such
as cryogenics.
Visit this site
for excellent
information on
a futuristic topic.

172

Dear Diary
http://www.mydeardiary.com

If you ever thought you or your diary were boring then just read these entries and think again.

I Love Cheese
http://www.ilovecheese.com

A lot of people like cheese, but how many really love it? Enough to eat a Wisconsin Aged Cheddar Cheese Ice Cream? Guides, recipes and links for the total cheese fanatic.

173

Sea Monkeys
http://www.seamonkeyworship.com

If you can't remember these, then visit this site for everything you could ever want to know about these strange creatures.

Mr Potato Head
http://www.mrpotatohead.net

Featuring facts and figures and a biography of Mr Potato Head himself. A tasty site for the spud you love.

174

Sodaplay Zoo
http://www.sodaplay.com/ constructor/index.htm

Create and animate your own imaginary creatures here, then place them in the 'Sodaplay Virtual Zoo' for others to admire!

Surfing Sobriety Test
http://www.turnpike.net/ ~mirsky/drunk/test1.html

Are you sober enough to be surfing the net? Take this test to find out. Hope you don't see double!

175

Paper Dolls
http://www.opdag.com

Including tips on how to get your paper dolls published and their history – this is the only place to come for all the info on...yes!...paper dolls!

Plane Sailing
http://www.paperairplanes.co.uk

Most people content themselves with the standard 'dart' model, but if you want a paper plane that out-flies all the rest, here's the low-down on the origami required.

**The World Federation
of the Right to Die Societies**
http://www.finalexit.org/world.fed.html

As the title suggests, this site is
dedicated to the intensely serious
subject of euthanasia.
It offers lots of
information about
the laws of
different countries
and tries to
answer some
difficult questions.

177

The Picasso Conspiracy
http://web.org.uk/picasso

An extensive site concerning the discovery and suppression of Picasso's 'Unknown Masterpiece', a secret work from 1934, full of occult imagery.

Peculiar Poetry
http://pages.total.net/~fishnet/poems.html

Read this very esoteric poetry and if you dare, buy one of Mr Mental patient's Products and you too could have verse dedicated to you.

Warning!
http://www.aviationpics.de

Ho-hum! One minute you are sitting on the beach enjoying the sunshine and minding your own business, the next, an aircraft skims the top of your head! Don't believe me?

Incredible Stuff I Made
http://www.cockeyed.com/incredible/incredible.html

Rob's page of incredible stuff he's made from frankly very limited resources. A banana skin coat, for example. And a cat coffin.

179

Bork, Bork, Bork!
http://www.rinkworks.com/dialect

Featuring 'The Dialectizer', this funny site allows you to change your dialect! Now you too can sound like a character from The Muppet Show!

Eric's Emotions
http://www.emotioneric.com

Request an emotion at this site and Eric will do his best to act it out for you. There is already a fantastically long list to choose from!

180

Poison Ivy Rash Hall Of Fame
http://www.poison-ivy.org/rash/index.htm

A gallery of submitted pictures showing the perils of coming into contact with poison ivy. Some of the pictures are truly disgusting, but if you've ever had a poison ivy incident yourself, here's where to share your pain.

Don't Give a Fig?
http://www.godhatesfigs.com

If you do too, you can join in their write-in campaign and read terrifying fig-related disaster stories.

The Bureau of Atomic Tourism
http://www.atomictourist.com

Do you fancy a trip to a nuclear
test site? Or perhaps you would rather
visit a place where the bombs are
actually made? This site
gives you the
low-down on all
things atomic!

Weird Virology
**http://www.virology.net/
WeirdVirology.html**

This web site takes a look at some of the
biggest diseases threatening us and
some of the weird 'cures' on offer.

The Darwin Awards
http://www.darwinawards.com

Responsible for 'commemorating the
remains of individuals who contributed
to the improvement of our gene pool by
killing themselves in really stupid ways'.

Circus Trees
http://www.bonfantegardens.com/trees/treesa.html

View pictures of wonders woven from living wood, creating trees in the shape of hearts, lightning bolts and rings.

High Tech Begging
http://www.geocities.com/Heartland/Bluffs/8105/index.html

He's homeless, hungry,half-drunk, unemployed,dumbas a rock and broke!! Do you fancy sending hima donation?

184

The Dull Men's Club
http://www.dullmen.com

There had to be a place on the Internet for dull men – and here it is! Marvel at what the 'dullest of dull' men do in their spare time.

Klingon
http://www.kli.org

Some people take television very seriously. Visit this hilarious site to find out everything a Trekkie would want to know about Klingonese!

Regia Anglopum
http://www.regia.org

If you would like to dress up as a Viking every weekend, then this is the place to come...

Take a Drive
http://www.webtruck.org/webtruck

Jump on board and take the toy truck for a spin. You can go backwards and forwards, load and unload marbles, and see the view from the on-board camera. Good, clean interactive fun!

Shake It Hammy!
http://www.hamsterdance.com

They are all here – dancing aliens, lizards, cows and even armadillos! Dance the night away with them in style!

Mind Your Head!
http://www.dartbase.com

Darts is a serious business – not just an old British pub game. Read the tips and improve your throw at this sharp site.

5

Celebrity Weirdness

Jerry Springer World
http://www.jerryspringertv.com/

You know you want to! Visit the official site of the Springer show to find out all about the wacky show topics and the man himself – you can even send him an e-mail!

Celebrity Astrology
http://celebrity.astrology.com/

When you just have to find out what sun sign Tom Cruise is, or Pamela Anderson, or Brad Pitt, or...

Famous Heights
http://www.famousheights.com

Do you lie awake at night wondering how tall your favorite celebrity is in real life? If so, you should definitely stop by this site.

Famous Quotations
http://www.famous-quotations.com

Check out the most interesting, funny and profound quotations from famous people throughout history. Guess who said, 'A jury consists of 12 persons chosen to decide who has the better lawyer'.

190

Celebrity Match
http://www.celebmatch.com/ bestmatch.php

Find which celebrity would most empathize with your point of view.

Former Child Star Central
http://members.tripod.com/ ~former_child_star/index.html

Visit this site to find out just what happened to those cute and not-so-cute kids who used to be famous on TV and in the movies. Whatever did happen to Corey Haim?

Return of the Muppets
http://www.muppets.com

TV's top puppets review their favorite web sites. There's games galore and you can find out what Miss Piggy is up to at the moment!

Skinema – Dermatology in the Movies
http://www.skinema.com

A funny site with a serious message... here you can find lots of details about how *not* to look after your skin.

192

Men Who Look Like Kenny Rogers.
http://www.
menwholooklikekennyrogers.com

After a certain age, a lot of men start to look like Kenny Rogers. So many that this site has had to close to new submissions. But there's almost 1,000 photos in the picture gallery, a guide on How To Look Like Kenny and, um, a corn muffin recipe.

Celebrities Exposed
http://celebrities.fun.ms/

See how the famous look when they aren't expecting a photo shoot!

Houses of the Rich and Famous
http://www.hollywoodusa.co.uk/celebrity-homes.htm

Would you like to find a celebrity mansion? This is where you will find all the stars' addresses! Now you just need a map and a cup and you can go round and ask to borrow some sugar.

194

Court TV Online
http://www.courttv.com/trials/famous
Read all about world-famous court cases, past and present, on this site run by America's Court TV station.

Last Words
http://www.geocities.com/ Athens/Acropolis/6537
Find out what presidents, philosophers, writers and famous business people had to say on their deathbeds!

Celebrity Site of the Day
http://www.csotd.com

A different celebrity site is listed every day here, and you can also see an archive going back to 1996. Your favorite celeb is sure to be here somewhere!

Celebrity Palace
http://www.celebritypalace.com

Come here for biographies, photos and fun facts on a wide range of celebrities, plus links to other celebrity web sites.

Who?
http://www.who2.com

A search page for famous people – this site provides links to fan sites, official sites and other useful information about the stars we love to love.

Nobel Peace Prize Winners
http://www.almaz.com/nobel

Covering the categories of literature, physics, chemistry, peace, economics, physiology and medicine – this is your chance to find out all about the Nobel laureates of our time.

Showbiz news!
http://movies.go.com

One of the best sites on the Net to find out what's hot and what's not in the world of movies and music. Check out your favorite celebrity or just read the news and gossip!

The Dead Musician Directory
http://elvispelvis.com/fullerup.htm

'A site about dead musicians…and how they got that way'. You can search by name or by cause of death, and there's even a latest late musicians section.

Star Spotting in Hollywood
http://www.seeing-stars.com

Everything you've ever wanted to know about where the stars play, work and live. Also find out about famous Hollywood landmarks and streets.

Arched Eyebrows
http://www.eyebrowz.com

This site offers do-it-yourself templates so that you can recreate the furry but feminine arches of stars such as Demi Moore, Gillian Anderson, Ingrid Bergman and Helena Bonham-Carter.

Celebrity Collectables
http://www.celebritycollectables.com

Authentic last wills and testaments, divorce files and autopsy files relating to your favorite celebrities.

Celebrity Screensavers and Wallpaper
http://www.celebrity-wallpaper.com

Just what you've always wanted – a picture of your favorite star that you can download and install on your computer screen. You need never miss them again!

Famous Birthdays
http://www.famousbirthdays.com

Find out which famous people were born on the same day as you...you might be surprised!

Celebrity Baby Names
http://www.infoplease.com/spot/celebrity-baby-names.html

Look up your favorite celebrities at this site and find out what exotic, strange and, sometimes, ridiculous names they give to their offspring.

Celebrity Death Pools
http://stiffs.com

A twisted but amusing site that lets you dabble in a little virtual gambling. Who do you think will push up the daisies next?

The Celebrity Café
http://www.thecelebritycafe.com

This online magazine features celebrity interviews, music reviews, travel stories, and more. There's loads to see here!

E-mail Santa
http://www.santaclaus.com
All-year-round e-mail access to the jolly, red-suited man himself.

New Line Cinema Auction
http://www.newline.com/nlcauction/upcoming/
Newline Films regularly auction off costumes and props from their latest films – here's your chance to own Austin Powers' suit or Freddy Krueger's Leather Blade Glove.

The Internet Movie Database
http://us.imdb.com

A huge site offering movie news, information and reviews. Your one-stop shop for everything movie-related.

Famous Mug-Shots
http://www.mugshots.org

Sometimes they just can't help themselves and end up behind bars! This small but entertaining site shows you the actual prison mugshots of some small and many big names.

204

Celebrity Love

**http://www.jokesandhumor.com/
tests/celebrity-love-match/**

Ever wanted to know which star you're
compatible with? Or wanted to know
which celebrity is your
true love match?
Answer this quiz
and find your
famous soulmate.

205

Hollywood Gossip and Chat
http://www.thehollywoodgossip.com/

For all the latest news and gossip about the stars. This is the site in the know!

Who's Alive – Who's Dead?
http://dpsinfo.com/dps/

Covering actors, musicians, athletes, politicians and more – this site gives the real low-down on who is still breathing and who isn't. A good site for settling arguments between friends!

206

The Obsessive Fan Sites Reviewed
http://www.ggower.com/fans

This site tracks down obsessive fan sites for different celebrities and gives awards for the most extreme and ridiculous.

The Celebrity Almanac
http://celebrityalmanac.com

If you really want to know what's happening in celebrity-land, this cool site is definitely the place to come. It's packed with fascinating information – for example, did you know that Cheryl Ladd's real name is Cheryl Stoppelmoor?

Find a Celebrity Site
http://www.celebrity-link.com

Want to find web sites dedicated to
your favorite celeb? The searchable
database on this site contains over 5,600
celebrities and has a total of more than
22,000 links.

Celebrity Golf
http://www.celebritygolf.com

You'd be surprised who enjoys a round
of golf. Alice Cooper for example.
Exclusive interviews and links to other
sites featuring celebrities and golf.

Famous Left-handers
**http://www.indiana.edu/
~primate/left.html**

Included in this site are details of left-handed artists, actors, musicians, athletes and US Presidents.

The Millionaire Magazine
http://www.millionaire.com

Containing real information aimed at real millionaires, this online magazine charts the fortunes of the richest amongst us and features luxury goods and even an auction.

Celebrity Recipes
http://www.recipegoldmine.com/celeb /celeb.html

If you fancy nibbling Katharine Hepburn's brownies, swallowing Nixon's meatloaf or getting your hands on William Shatner's muffins, here's your site!

Celebrity Death Match
http://www.mtv.com/onair/deathmatch

The homepage of the television series of the same name. Come to this site to see the two Mansons or the Spice Girls battle it out in the ring.

The TV Single Dad's Hall of Fame
http://www.tvdads.com

They are a small but worthy minority, coping courageously with kids, dogs, and their own love lives. They are...single dads on TV.

Entertainment Online
http://www.eonline.com

The homepage of entertainment, featuring gossip, news, links to celebrities and much more. A good place to start a search.

Oprah Online
http://www.oprah.com

The queen of chat shows has her own web site! There's fun details on the show itself and also links to self-help articles.

The Celebrity Zone
http://www.celebrityzone.co.uk

This site provides photographs and information on all your favorite celebrities. Included are movie stars, pop stars, models, sports stars and TV stars. Test your celebrity knowledge with the quiz.

The National Enquirer Online
http://www.jossip.com

Celebrity plus media plus Mahattan is a heady mix. Enjoy all the latest chat including updates from The National Enquirer.

The Right Royal Family
http://www.royal.gov.uk

This is the official site of the British monarchy – not too much gossip available here but an excellent all-round resource for information, including photos and the history of the royals.

Hollywood.com
http://www.hollywood.com

The name says it all. This is a huge site and search engine for all things Hollywood. If you are looking for news or gossip, you'll definitely find it here.

Celebrity Games
http://www.celebritygame.com

Want to play a game with your favorite celebrity? Well, now you can! This cool site has free online jigsaw puzzles and other games featuring the celebrities of your choice!

Chic Happens
http://www.hintmag.com

Who wears what and where? The inside gossip on celebrity fashion.

Annoying Celebs
http://www.newgrounds.com/assassin/

Are you sick of sycophantic celebrity sites? Then if you fancy virtually assassinatinating a star then release that aggression and go for it - but it's all legal and online only.

215

Biography Section
http://www.sanantonio.gov/library/web/biography.asp

This site contains links to biographies of artists, musicians, politicians and many major historical figures. Brush up on your knowledge and learn about these great figures from the past.

Great Women
http://www.greatwomen.org

The National Women's Hall of Fame seeks to honor women of achievement. Search their growing database of high-flying females, or nominate a new entry yourself.

I Wanna Be Famous
http://www.iwannabefamous.com

Making ordinary people famous one person at a time. Submit a photo and profile and get your 15 minutes of fame.

Quote – Unquote
http://fly.to/quoteunquote

Here you'll find quotes from celebrities on a variety of subjects. Who do you think admitted 'In the gym, I only wear black and diamonds'?

Time Magazine's Top 100
http://www.pathfinder.com/ time/time100/index.html

We all have an opinion on the most influential figures of the 20th century – find out who *Time Magazine* voted for.

218

Warp Factor
http://www.allfunnypictures.com/warp.html

Be it george Bush or Hugh Grant, take a face, move your mouse and warp them to your heart's content.

Pop-culture Junk Mail
http://www.popculturejunkmail.com

This site offers links to pop culture-themed web sites with a bias towards British royalty, movies, the 1980s and much more.

219

The Weird Site
http://www.theweirdsite.com/

There's weird news, weird facts and
weird freebies on this site. Check it out!

The Fame Tracker Almanac
http://www.fametracker.com

A cornucopia of gossip, tidbits and
news. A stylish site that tracks the
movements of the stars so you don't
have to.

Celebrity Stock Exchange
http://www.bbc.co.uk/celebdaq

Use your skill and judgement to buy and sell 'shares' in celebrities. Every week the shares you own will pay out a dividend depending on how much press coverage your celebs receive!

Search a Celeb
http://www.celebhoo.com

A search engine for finding out everything about the celebrity of your choice. A good place to start in your hunt for trivia, gossip or celebrity news.

221

Pitt of Horror
http://www.pittofhorror.com

Let horror movie legend, Ingrid Pitt, tell you all about the latest horror happenings and news from around the world. Oh, and you can join her spooky fan club too!

Famous Vegetarians
http://www.famousveggie.com

Find out which of the rich and famous don't eat meat. You can also browse recipes and find out how to make vegan chocolate pudding.

Make His Day
http://www.clinteastwood.net

Loads of top Clint Eastwood stuff here. You can even download a message for your telephone answering machine!

Biographical Dictionary
http://www.s9.com/biography

This is a searchable site containing a gigantic database of notable men and women who have shaped our world, from ancient times to the present.

Dalai Lama
http://www.dalailama.com/

For some spiritual teachings and direction in this celebrity-driven world, consult His Holiness.

The Pope
http://www.vatican.va

No, you're not mistaken – the Pope is online! This is his official web site where you can read articles and find out about papal blessings.

Celebrity Diaries
http://www.diarist.net/links/
celebritydiaries.shtml

Celebrity diaries and biogs from the likes of Anna Kournikova, William Shatner and Ian McKellen.

Famous Cats and Dogs
http://www.citizenlunchbox.com/
famous/animals.html

Can't think of that cartoon cat you used to love? Need some naming ideas for your pets? This is the place to come.

This Movie Sucks!
http://www.mrcranky.com

Mr Cranky always finds reasons to object to the latest movie releases. You won't believe what he gets away with!

Hair Today, Gone Tomorrow
http://www.celebrity-hairstyles.org/

If you want a hairstyle you've seen on your favourite celeb just consult these photos, take it along to your hairdresser and you too can look like a million dollars.

Rubber Faces
http://www.rubberfaces.com

Have fun playing with celebrity 'rubber' faces! Give them giant foreheads, fat lips and strange eyes. Over 80 celebrity faces to choose from, including Bill Gates, Sarah Michelle Geller and Michael J Fox. And a gallery with some of the highlights.

227

Weird Celebrities
http://funny-town.blogspot.com/ 2006/12/10-most-bizarre- celebrities_28.html

If you think you need talent to be a star then just look at the top 10 of bizarre celebrities!

Write for Hollywood
http://www.donedealpro.com/ default.aspx

Got an idea for the next big blockbuster movie? Check out this site for all the latest scriptwriting advice and gossip.

228

A Celeb on Your Desktop
http://www.celebritydesktop.com

Do you have a favorite celebrity?
Then why not install him or her on
your computer permanently as a
screensaver or wallpaper? There are
thousands of free downloads here, from
Angelina Jolie to Michael Jackson!

Film Flaws
http://www.moviecliches.com

Listed by topic, this fab web site
contains the most common and
annoying celluloid clichés.

229

Psychic Stars
http://www.psychics.co.uk/celebrities/

Celebrities are a sensitive bunch, dso no surprise that they've had psychic experiences – details here.

Barefoot Celebrities!
http://members.tripod.com/ ~a_spring/barefoot2.html

This little site is devoted to the bare feet of the rich and famous, from Tori Amos to Jon Bon Jovi. Just be grateful you can't smell them too!

Ape Culture
http://www.apeculture.com

This strange site is dedicated to 'popular culture and the stripmall life'. It includes concert and movie reviews, celebrity news and features, all with a distinctly off-the-wall flavor.

Who's Buried Where?
http://www.findagrave.com

Do you have a burning desire to find out where Gene Kelly and other stars are buried? If so, check this out – you can even buy the T-shirt!

231

TV Ark
http://www.tv-ark.org.uk
Superb British TV nostalgia site with a vast array of info, pictures, theme tunes and loads more. Search by channel or by genre.

Juggle Baby!
http://www.juggling.org/movies

Did you know that over 350 known films contain scenes of juggling? What films did Robert de Niro and Johnny Depp juggle in? Log on to find out.

Celebrities Distorted
http://www.quirked.com/distortions

Countless photos of celebrity photos distorted for comic effect. Includes an A-Z search to find your favourite celeb.

233

6

UFOs and Aliens

Anomalous Space Images and UFOs
http://www.anomalous-images.com/index.html

Is there a face on Mars? This site offers photographs and information on this anomaly and many others.

The Center for UFO Studies
http://www.cufos.org/index.html

A general overview of UFO sightings in history – and there's even a page where you can report your very own sighting!

UFOs and the Church
http://www.logoschristian.org/sightings/

This site contains a list of religious leaders and their sightings. They know they're real!

UFO Watchtower
http://www.ufowatchtower.com

This purpose-built watchtower in Hooper, Colorado just might give you your best chance of spotting a flying saucer! But then again, it might not.

Cosmic Conspiracies
http://www.ufos-aliens.co.uk

A general site about UFOs and aliens –
including film footage, photographs, a
chat room, information on government
conspiracies and the latest news.

Is There a Military Cover-up?
http://www.ufoevidence.org/topics/
Government.htm

This site examines the UFO encounters
with the military and the conspiracy to
keep it all quiet.

237

How to Fake Your Own Alien Autopsy

http://www.trudang.com/autopsy.html

A lighter look at the business of dissecting aliens – including bleeps and blunders and a 'How To Make An Alien' Handbook.

Astrobiology at NASA

http://astrobiology.arc.nasa.gov/ index.cfm

For a scientific look at the anomalies of space, planets and strange objects in the sky – visit the official NASA site.

238

MUFON – 'The Mutual UFO Network'
http://www.mufon.com

Have you been looking for an organization to join, one that provides hotlines, trains field investigators, and even hosts an annual convention? If so, MUFON could be the network for you.

239

UFO Folklore
http://www.artgomperz.com/mainpix.html

This site boasts a gallery of photographs and links to videos and the stories behind the sightings.

Above Top Secret
http://www.abovetopsecret.com

This site is dedicated to uncovering government conspiracies surrounding Area 51, aircraft projects, and the New World Order.

Saucer Smear
http://www.martiansgohome.com/smear

Reporting on the business of Ufology itself – the movers, the shakers and all the latest news and gossip.

Alien Message Board
http://www.scifichronicles.com/amb.htm

Amongst other features, there is an alien quiz, an alien shopping mall, and even an alien lonely hearts column ('Lonely, friendless, feel the need to breed? Find the alien of your dreams at the Alien Love Connection.')

The UFO Network
http://www.ufon.org

The UFO Network site charts UFO sightings from around the world. Check out the archive photos and decide for yourself whether or not they are hoaxes.

When Will We Have Warp Drives?
http://www.lerc.nasa.gov/ WWW/PAO/warp.htm

Dealing with the science and technology of travelling at the speed of light, this site is a fascinating attempt to answer the question.

To Debunk Or Not
http://www.ufoevidence.org/

Including dozens of articles and reports about UFO close encounters, photographs of anomalies, crop circles, alien abductions, and much much more, this site has it all.

UFO Abduction Insurance
http://www.ufo2001.com

This tongue-in-cheek site offers insurance against being abducted by aliens. A single lifetime premium of $19.95 will cover you to the tune of $10,000,000!

243

Thought Screen Helmet
http://www.stopabductions.com

Worried about being abducted by aliens? Help is at hand! This site takes you through how to build a useful thought screen helmet, step by step.

International UFO Museum and Research Center
http://www.roswellufomuseum.com/

This real-life museum offers details on the Roswell Incident and research articles. It even has a gift shop where you can purchase Area 51 golf balls!

UFO Art
**http://dcwi.com/~talpazan/
Welcome.html**

Homepage of a Romanian-born artist
who draws, paints and sculpts UFOs
and aliens.

UFO Anomalies Zone
**http://www.rense.com/general/
otherros.htm**

You've probably not heard of
Kecksburg, where the government
cover-up was more successful than
Roswell. Find out the truth about the
giant acorn that fell from the sky.

245

SETI – 'The Search for Extraterrestrial Intelligence'
http://www.seti.org

The official homepage of the SETI Institute. An extremely interesting and worthy site with all the information on the current search projects – and don't forget to check out 'SETI @ Home', where you can help them search from your very own computer!

Aliens Beneath Our Feet
http://www.reptoids.com

Reptiles evolved into reptilian-humanoid beings called Reptoids which live underground. But might be able to pilot UFOs on the side.

Alien Biology
http://www.planetarybiology.com/

Visit this site for fascinating scientific details about the possibility and specifics of life on other planets!

247

Bob Lazar
http://www.boblazar.com

Bob Lazar has made many claims that he was employed at Area 51. This is his web site – perhaps he is telling the truth!

Shooting Stars For Sale
http://www.theskyisfalling.com

Own a piece of the moon for $5000 plus shipping. This site will sell you a rare meteorite, complete with owner's manual. Ships worldwide.

Great Dreams
http://www.greatdreams.com/ufos.htm

Boasting links to 2,803 sites on a variety of UFO topics, this site must be visited by all fans of the 'greys'.

Zerotime
http://www.zerotime.com/ufo

Including the likely home of The Grey Aliens (Zeta 2 Reticuli) and NASA's official document explaining what procedures to follow when encountering aliens.

The UFO Museum
http://unmuseum.mus.pa.us/ufo.htm

Read about the history of strange
happenings in the sky in the Hall of UFO
Mysteries – a gallery of the Unnatural
Museum.

The Black Vault
http://www.blackvault.com

Containing a huge list of links, this is one
of the Internet's best sites on all things to
do with UFOs, alien cover-ups and
government conspiracies. A must-see
site for die-hard UFO or conspiracy fans.

250

Zeta Talk
http://www.zetatalk.com

According to this site, aliens visit the Earth regularly! Discover why we are gradually getting acquainted with our visitors from outer space, and what needs to happen to allow the process to occur faster.

All About UFOs
http://ufos.about.com/mbody.htm

Get the latest news of UFO sightings around the world, by courtesy of the giant About.com web site.

251

Nuts About UFOs
http://www.ufonut.com

This site contains historical accounts, photos and links in an irreverent style.

Alien Dating Service?
http://www.alienlovebite.com

Ever fallen in love with someone you shouldn't have fallen in love with? It may be that an alien abducted you and programmed you to respond to another abductee. Find out all about this bizarre theory on this site.

The US National
UFO Reporting Center
http://www.nwlink.com/~ufocntr

Whilst only covering the US and
Canada, this site still contains some
fascinating details of

recent case studies
including the
fascinating sighting
over Illinois at the
start of the new
millennium.

253

UFO Alert
http://www.UFOAlert.com

Engaged in the task of documenting UFO sightings from around the world, this site is a must-see in your quest to uncover the truth.

Meteorite Central
http://meteoritecentral.com

For the latest news and views about lumps of rock, and other things, that fall from the sky, this is the place to go. The site includes a mailing list as well as a bulletin board.

UFO City
http://www.ufocity.com
Another vast and regularly-updated site offering 'hot-off-the-press' news, many links and articles about UFOs, a bulletin board, a 'watch' campaign, and much more.

The UFO Reports' Archive
http://www.geocities.com/ Area51/Rampart/2653/reports.html
In this massive archive of postings from the Alt.UFO newsgroup, you can read hundreds of reports of UFO sightings.

The Oz Files
http://www.theozfiles.com/index.html

Do UFO's fly upside down, down under?
This site provides an Antipodean
perspective on the UFO scene,
including possible UFO connections with
Australian Aboriginal culture.

Project 1947
http://www.project1947.com

Project 1947 takes a closer look at the
UFO phenomenon that began at this
time in our history, offering details and
photographs of the main UFO sightings.

Six Inexplicable Encounters
http://www.popularmechanics.com/science/air_space/1282476.html

As suggested by the title, this web site takes a detailed look at six UFO encounters from around the world that have stumped the skeptics.

International UFO Congress
http://www.ufocongress.com

Would you like to know when the next UFO congress is held and how you can be updated on the discussions? Check out this site for all these details and more.

Aliens as Ancestors
http://theroad1.tripod.com

Are UFOs and aliens really our ancestors
checking up on us? Visit this site for
images and descriptions of extra-
terrestrial encounters throughout history,
and puzzling references from the Bible.

Alien Abduction
http://www.abduct.com

Personal experiences of alien
abduction from all over the world are
shared on this site.

Food for Thought
http://www.countdowncreations.com/ astronaut_space_food.htm

If you happen to be in space searching for alien life forms don't forget to take your astronaut food with you.

The Science Behind the 'X-Files'
http://huah.net/scixf

Taking a very close look at a few episodes of the popular TV show, this site offers an explanation for the X-Files science bits. An interesting read.

259

The Bible UFO Connection
http://www.bibleufo.com

A web site all about the theory that God travels the skies in a UFO, and Multi-National Corporations are implicated in a plot to make us fear aliens so that we will shoot down the UFO that Jesus is going to be flying back to earth in.

The Lunar Embassy
http://www.lunarembassy.com

How would you like to buy a piece of the moon or Mars? This is precisely what this site offers.

HR Giger
http://www.hrgiger.com

This is the official site of Mr HR Giger, the genius artist who created the visual horror of the xenomorphe in the 'Alien' trilogy of movies. His art is sinister and yet beautiful – a must-see site for fans of science fiction and art.

UFO Sightings in the UK
http://www.mysteriousbritain.co.uk/ufo's/ufolist1.html

A neatly designed site documenting and updating UFO sightings specific to the United Kingdom from 793AD.

Alien Dave
http://www.aliendave.com/aliendave.html

A huge array of conspiracy theories are detailed on this site, most of them not surprisingly involving aliens. And a man called Dave.

Are You an Abductee?
**http://www.robotpegasys.com/
alienswfs/a.html**

Answer the quiz questions to find out if
you are one of the select few!

Possible UFO Crash Sites
and Retrievals
**http://www.cseti.com/
crashes/crash.htm**

A huge international list of UFO crash
site locations and the possible discovery
of dead aliens. Has there been one
near you? – log on to find out.

263

Alien Shopping
http://www.ufomall.com

All the alien-related merchandise you could ever need is available for purchase here!

Alien Autopsy News.
http://www.v-j-enterprises.com/ jroswell.html

All the latest developments in the controversy over the Roswell Alien Autopsy tape.

The Mystical Universe
http://mysticaluniverse.com

A general site reporting various paranormal phenomena including the very latest UFO sightings, alien abductions, hauntings and NASA news.

Life On Mars
http://www.enterprisemission.com/

Richard Hoagland's mission is to make NASA admit there is life on Mars and our Moon. He claims there is evidence and it should be in the public domain. See for yourself.

The Time Travel Research Center
http://www.time-travel.com

As the title suggests, this site offers fascinating information about the history, the science, and the possibilities of travelling through time.

The Paranormal News
http://www.paranormalnews.com

Updated frequently and with great video footage, this site highlights news stories about strange happenings in the sky and other paranormal events.

SARA – 'The Society of Amateur Radio Astronomers'
http://www.bambi.net/sara.html
The site to visit if you want to set up your own backyard radio telescope or just meet other like-minded people from around the globe. An excellent resource.

267

What Are The Triangles?
http://keyholepublishing.com/
What_Are_The_Triangles.htm

This online report discusses sightings of 'impossible' crafts, and provides photos, testimonies and links to other sites discussing triangle-shaped craft.

Angry Alien
http://www.angryalien.com

This site not only shows the film, Alien being re-enacted by cartoon bunnies, but also shows other famous films featuring cartoon bunny actors!

268

Bad Astronomy
http://www.badastronomy.com

Explains the flawed astronomy featured in films, on TV and in the news, including discussions about The Apollo Moon Hoax, Planet X and The Face On Mars.

Alien Journal
http://www.ufomagazine.co.uk/

The nearest thing to a gossip mag about aliens. Easy-to-read and maybe it'll prepare you for the invasion.

Committee for Skeptical Enquiry
http://www.csicop.org

You can search the site for a variety of articles on UFOs and aliens, as well as other 'fringe' subjects.

Close-minded Science
http://www.amasci.com/ weird/wclose.html

An interesting collection of articles about scientific skepticism generally – when to believe, when to debunk.

270

Alien Abduction Photos
http://www.rense.com/general32/abduct.htm

Amazing-looking photos of the aftermath of a Brazilian man being abducted from his bed through the ceiling into a spaceship.

Kiddy Culture
http://aliensandchildren.org/

Simply a vast resource of links and articles on all things UFO-related. A good place to start your own investigation.

West to Mars
http://www.marswest.org

This site gives an artistic impression of human colonization of the red planet.

Extraterrestrials – What Are They Like?
http://www.geocities.com/ Area51/Shadowlands/6583/et.html

A huge site dedicated to the task of categorizing and describing alien life forms – including a series of interesting articles about the impact of aliens landing on Earth.

272

The Languages of Other Worlds
http://www.neuvel.net/alienlang.htm

How do you sing the Ewok celebration song. Learn here – but only if you want to.

Mission to Mars
http://www.androidpubs.com

The web site for a manned mission to Mars, for which tickets are available now for a mere $2,000,000. The departure date is July 15, 2018, due in to Mars on August 21, 2018 if the traffic's not too bad...

273

Alien Alley Art Gallery
http://www.alienalley.com

Online gallery of UFO-related art. You don't have to have been abducted to exhibit here, but it helps.

Scary Aliens
http://www.xenomorph.org

This claims to be the first and largest site on the net to deal exclusively with collectibles from the Alien films. Whether you want a copy of the original movie posters or a model alien of your very own, this is the place to come!

Top Secret!
http://accelerationresearch.tripod.com

This site explores the many mysteries surrounding the Aurora, including whether it may be responsible for some presumed UFO sightings.

Roswell
http://ds.dial.pipex.com/ritson

With eye-witness accounts, stills from the famous film, and more – this unbiased site is an excellent place to find out the facts about the Roswell Incident.

275

42

http://www.bbc.co.uk/cult/hitchhikers/

A tribute to the cult that Douglas Adams spawned. The Hitch-hiker's Guide to the Galaxy gives the answers to life, the universe and everything.

Area 51 Trip Report
http://www.area51zone.com

With photographs of Area 51 and various 'alleged' aircraft, this site takes an objective look at this famous conspiracy.

Alien Bases
http://www.karinya.com/bases1.htm

An up-to-date map of all the alien bases on Earth - really.

Atlantis
http://www.world-famous.com/DavidHamelStuff/

David Hamel has been told by aliens the truth about ancient architecture, the Bible, the Dead Sea Scrolls, Atlantis, the Pyramids, Stonehenge, and many other theories! Let him convince you too.

UFO Sightings by Astronauts
http://www.anomalous-images.com/astroufo.html

Many US astronauts claim to have seen UFOs during their space missions. Read about the sightings here, in some cases with previously unpublished photographs.

Afrer care
http://www.intrudersfoundation.org/ acs.html

Have you been probed? Seek help here!

Unknown Country
http://www.unknowncountry.com

This is the web site of author Whitley Strieber, who famously claimed to have been abducted and experimented upon by aliens. Read here about the latest mysteries he is investigating.

279

LAGOON WEB SITE

Games, Books, Puzzles and Gizmos

Visit the Lagoon Web Site to view a
staggering range of fantastic games,
puzzles and books to suit all.

www.thelagoongroup.com

And if those 500 weren't enough you either need to kill some more time at

http://www.killsometime.com/pictures/ pictures.asp

or you've lost your marbles!

http://members.tripod.com/
~abnorml/A.HTM